T0207690

RAPED IN THE CHURCH

MOHADEEBAH

authorHOUSE®

AuthorHouse™
1663 Liberty Drive
Bloomington, IN 47403
www.authorhouse.com
Phone: 1 (800) 839-8640

Published by AuthorHouse 11/11/2019

ISBN: 978-1-7283-3500-1 (sc)
ISBN: 978-1-7283-3499-8 (e)

RAPED IN THE CHURCH

This book is not intended for everyone to read or for everyone to like; it is for the millions of people who have been unjustly raped in the church, without any type of human justice or foreseeable biblical justice. This book is for those who have been hurt or abused in the natural, psychological, mental, physical, and the spiritual realm.

If you are a new convert, do not read this book, because some things may shock you or even shake your faith in your local lay members or clergy, who do not deserve any unjust criticism. Some stories may seem unreal but they are based on real life events of everyday people who you see or are seen in the sanctuary worshiping God never knowing what they are going through or why they leave the church today, some even convert to other religions. As a result of hurt and frustration many never return to the organized church and prefer a relationship with God through television evangelist.

I am not targeting Christianity but most of the stories and events are from people who are or once was a Christian, I must say in all fairness I must say that I'm a Christian and this book is written from a Christian point of view. It's written to heal as well as inform that not everyone in the church is of the church, meaning the kingdom of God. To the clergy and lay members please remember this the Lord said (woe unto the Shepherd that scatter MY Sheep), he said that we are the sheep of his pasture. Many people in leadership today seem to forget that very important fact, that we are not theirs to command and bid as they see fit. If you choose to read this book, you will always have an awareness of what is going on with those who have been spiritually raped. Some people may not believe you when you tell them what you have read and what you learned which is fine. Remember they did not believe Jesus either. Finally as one pastor once said to me many years ago (that education stuff isn't going to get you anywhere), he/she didn't know that the bible has been translated by some of the best scholars of our time, and our theology has had may contributors throughout history. From the Quakers, Shakers, Lutheran, Catholic, Jews, and even Mormons. The lord said that knowledge would steadily increase, and if a man lacks knowledge or wisdom let him ask God who gives limberly and upbraids not.

PREFACE

In this book, I'm not trying to provide you with a new way of thinking or change your mind about any church. In fact, I refuse to focus on or mention any denomination. It is my hope that we can help you by showing you that God is able to use our circumstances and adversity too glorify him or make you stronger.

Some things will make you stronger in your faith in or toward God; you can survive being raped in the church.

Even though it's a subject not talked about in many churches today, it does happen, and many people don't return because of it. Many being hurt for so many years ask questions ex: (God how you can allow this happen to me, what did I do wrong. It's not necessarily that you did anything wrong; maybe god is teaching you to hear his voice or teaching you to lean and depend on him and not men. Remember he said cursed is every man that trust in the arm of flesh. Remember you must be teachable, if you can't receive any advice or critics, you must examine yourself. The apostle Paul said to lower yourself or join yourself to men of low esteem, and to esteem your brother higher than yourself. Always someone can teach you something if you're able to receive what the Lord God is saying. Its prayer that the Lord God would open your understanding so that you won't be swept away with every wind and doctrine and that you will learn to hear the voice of God for yourself.

Finally, the Lord Jesus was a man in the flesh who had emotions and feelings like you and I, he felt things.

He cried and felt pain even the sting of betrayal by the people he was the closest to; but praise be to God he kept on dying for me and for you. Don't give up on the church, because God never gave up and he never will until the day of redemption.

A WORD OF THANKS

Many people have had a great influence on me and, have helped me make many life changing decision. One person who comes to mind first is Pastor Drake of F.B.H.C who said God has a greater calling on your life, at a time when I was questioning my own self-worth and purpose in the kingdom of God. Thanks to Bishop N.J. Roach who proved what a bishop is supposed to be like and exemplifying the character of God in all the fruit of the spirit; when I met you I finally understood what it meant when the disciple said did not our hearts burn while he spoke with us. To Pastor E. Smith who brought me into the fold of Jesus Christ, even if I don't say it I still take a part of you with me, without you I never would have even started to search for the deeper things in the word of God. To Pastor M.P Dunbar who taught us never to give up and too praise God no matter what you're going through, for that, I give you much respect. To the ministers at New Jerusalem you helped me express myself as a man of God and express myself in spiritual things. It's not so much of what you said but the life that you lived and the little things that you did for one another, and to Pastor A. Simpkins thank you for taking a broken person who was wounded by the church and teaching me that sometimes you need professional help.

To all those who corrected me in many of my former teachings that were wrong, you could have raked me over the coals but you didn't, you showed me kindness, and understanding. You taught me no matter what you don't give up on the one you love, even if it means doing some unorthodox things. To my mom and dad who were married for thirty seven years before she fell asleep in Christ, you had some very rocky moments, but you stayed together, thanks for the values, stories, and the constant family atmosphere. You brought us too Sunday school even though we didn't learn anything, and created a foundation. Mom, you stood strong when everyone else's children were committing themselves to Christ; you said it would be our decision when we were ready. To my dad thank you for being a man who did whatever it took to take care of his family thank you for showing me the value of a fathers touch and influence, and showing me how to show love even if you didn't say it that often.

And last and Greatest I want to thank my wife, friend, lover, helper, strength, my better half. Thank you for showing me what it means to forgive, those who constantly abused and used you. You have reminded me what it means to be humble and a lady at the same time. Without you I could not have made it through such a difficult period in my life when I had lost faith in God, just to look at you remind me of what God's grace really means. I didn't deserve you, but you chose to take a chance on this broken vessel, you chose to build this heart that was scattered and mended the pieces together again. Thank you for bringing me back to church to start all over again, you showed me the beauty and innocence with the simplicity of your faith. It's what I needed not some deep theological view or explanation, but the small things. You make me so happy without you this book could have never materialized. Babe you showed me how to laugh again, when I had forgot how to smile; you saw through that fake smile and ministered to the pain. For that I am truly grateful. Without you I should be dead today, you made me go to the doctor, and it's because you cared those checkups saved my life. Now I know I can be serious, laugh and be holy at the same time, I love you not because of what you do but in spite of everything, you do.

Love U Baby.

CHAPTER 1

BEFORE I GO ANY FURTHER, I would very much like to define Rape according to the state that I live in, once again, every state is different according to its laws and statues, but the state that I reside defines rape as having carnal knowledge of the female body. In this state it's impossible for a woman to rape a man, another woman or a child; hear me very clearly I'm not saying that it doesn't happen it does just not by definition. Therefore, what I'm about to discuss is rape in the spiritual. You may say what is rape in the spiritual realm, simply put its having knowledge of one's spiritual life, limits, frailties, and physiological make up and there use against that person to the benefit of another for fame, power, pride, financial gain or to deflect some personal wrong doing and make the other person appear in error. When we talk about rape, it brings up many emotions especially to those who have survived it or are working their way through it. There are very basic and appropriate emotions that we experience due to the attack, the reason I say appropriate is because emotions are valid it's just how we interpret them or choose to express them in public or in secret. God never condemns us for having emotions or experiencing emotions, only in how we react to them and what we do because of our emotions. Remember it was God himself who gave us emotions and we were created in his image, and at times, he even expressed emotions like, crying, laughing, anger, sorrow, rejection, heartbreak. These are just some small examples of the things that result as a reaction to our emotions. A physical rape occurs every day of every hour in this country, many go unreported due to feelings of shame, guilt, feeling dirty, worthless, or because it was committed by someone, they thought they could trust. Being in law enforcement you learn over time that most rapes are committed by someone who knows the victim or, has come in close contact with the victim, I'm not suggesting that they all occur in this manner, but based on my experience the majority of them do occur by someone they know. Spiritual rape usually occurs by someone the victim knows or someone having authority over them in some form, but unlike physical rape the victim of spiritual rape do get a chance to view there attacker before the offense is committed, if it were a reportable crime many of attackers would be in jail today. In my opinion it should be a crime to spiritually rape someone to rob them of their God given innocence and steal their faith in some cases. While writing this book I know I could go on and on about physical rape, but I will not for three central reasons, First I don't want to diminish or belittle in any way a horrific experience someone has had in their past. To survive the experience and live with it every day of your life is torment, without someone trying to write about it, and too not give her/him a voice to speak on it. I believe only the voice of a victim can truly speak too this horrible act. Secondly it would take hours to cover many aspects of rape and there are enough books out there on the subject. Finally, I want to talk about a part that the churches rarely if ever talk about in a direct manner. Because they are the attacker or don't know how to deal with someone who has been spiritually raped in the church. I know in writing this book it will cause me much grief and agony but I fear if we as the children of God don't address this subject there will many who will be raped and will never again return to the church for this reason, if this book can encourage people to have an open dialogue it would have been well worth my suffering. Rape is in my opinion one of the biggest causes of people leaving the church today it debilitates people emotionally, spiritually, and sometimes even physically. I am not a doctor of any type; but what I do write is based on actual conversations with victims of physical and spiritual rape. Through the course of many years, I've discovered many wonderful and painful truths about the churches today and the way God designed our wonderful bodies. I recall speaking with a woman who had been raped and she talked about how the physical scars healed but the mental scars remained for life. As human beings we can associate ourselves or disassociate our minds from physical pain, but mental pain is more difficult to separate oneself from, some people can suppress certain emotions, for long periods of time, but if a traumatic experience is not properly dealt with it can resurface in other areas of their life, Ex: suicide, misplaced anger, rage, fear, nervousness, and even physical break down of the body. As you continue to read if you can identify with any of the people who are mention in this book; please examine your conscience and see if there's any unresolved issues, and if you can't resolve them seek professional help.

CHAPTER 2

THE BEGINNING OF HOPE

DO YOU REMEMBER WHERE YOU were when you first received Christ in your life, do you recall how you felt how everything seemed to take on a new meaning and you finally understood that life had meaning. I like to think that my conversion into Christianity was unique and that no one else in the world had the same experience that I did. I can remember when I received Christ in my life, it felt like I could do anything that I wanted to do in Christ of course, if someone would have said cast out this demon in Jesus name at that time I would have tried it; believing that I could do all things through Christ, and that no weapon formed against me shall prosper. Scripture would have come to me on the spot like greater is he that is in me than he that is in the world. I was ready to go out and tell the world that Jesus had risen from the dead and he was coming back for his people, the joy and enthusiasm of what Christ has done for us how he died for our sins, was the greatest mystery I had ever heard and experienced in my life. Allow me to give you a little insight into my conversion to Christianity, my mother was saved by the grace of God and her mother was saved also along with my grandfather, which later helped build a holiness church, he later passed away before I got to know him, but to see his wife, my grandmother always helping someone else and having some type of prayer meeting at her house or some other lay members house it was a beautiful and a scary thing at the same time. You see my mother was a praying woman she believed in god and prayer, she never gave up on god or if she did, she never let us know it. I have some very fond memories of her, there is one that sticks out in my mind and will always remain vivid; as a child when my mother was in distress she knew how to pray, she would pray out loud calling on the name of Jesus.

She would pray like this in private and at prayer meetings she never changed a thing what you saw was pretty much what you got, that's one thing I admired about her even when people talked about her she would always treat them with kindness you would never know how she felt about them, if they were in need of something or someone to talk too she would be more than happy to lend a hand. I was forced to go to church what seemed like every Sunday or prayer meeting that was going on, even though I didn't learn a thing in Sunday school it laid a foundation in my life; a foundation that I would later come to depend on in my daily walk with Christ. You see my parents didn't know about theology or apologetics, that we practice today using commentaries were unheard of and never mentioned in our home, but one thing we did have was respect for God and our parents, and until this day, I believe they established a simple pattern of how our relationship should be with our heavenly father. As children we believed in God in a way that only children can understand a perfect example would be if one of us would do something to the other and we couldn't retaliate, we had a little song we would sing that said (God's going to get you for that ain't no need of running he knows where you at). Simple things like that would remind us that there is a God, and the prayers that my mother prayed for us were heard by him. I cannot go any further without mentioning how hard she prayed, sometimes for hours at time, I can remember on many occasions lying in the bed listening to her pray and sometimes I could even feel her prayers when she cried out for Jesus to save us and watch over us. She would pray so hard until I felt something resting on my body it felt like a shadowing presence that consumed my entire body as I lay there, and sometimes I would whisper silent prayers in my room as she prayed.

At that time, I didn't know about the personal Holy Spirit, we heard of people having it, but I never experienced it. Until this day I believe that her prayers played a big part in my salvation, without her example of being a saved woman of God I would have never been curious about Jesus or felt that something was missing in my life in my teen years. If you're a parent please don't give up on praying for your children it does work, but remember the bible teaches us that faith without works is dead, and don't be ashamed to confess your faith in their presence it's important your children know what you believe but also see what you believe. The apostle said faith come by hearing and hearing by the word of God how can they hear without a preacher and how can they preach except they be sent. As a result of seeing what my mother believed, in high school myself and a few friends would sit down and discuss the bible and what we thought we knew at the time there was always a hunger for something and the feeling that something was missing. Like most teenagers, I felt I wanted to experience life and do anything I was big and bad enough to do. If you haven't caught on yet I was no saint by any means in fact I was just the opposite, a child of Satan; even though I had a praying mother she never forced us to come too Christ, even though there were people in the church trying to force us to be saved, she said when you're ready it's your decision. Many of my friends and relatives were saved and filled with the

Holy Ghost and most of them went back to the youthful life they felt they missed, in the teenage years. Now I understand that you can't pressure people to be saved Jesus never pressured anyone to come to him he talked and allowed them to make up their own minds, even God in the new testament never forced mankind to love him he allowed them to reject him even though he created them from the earth. Now I understand what Jesus said when he said through love and kindness have, I drawn thee, he also said, and they will come to me and be taught of me and then they will be saved. We can't come to him unless we see him in the person of Jesus who loved us and died for us and wants the best for our soul; he wants to reconcile you back to God. Only when we understand, he is the only one, who can fill the void in our life, only then can we truly be happy.

When dealing with today's youth please keep this in mind, not all of your of friends were saved when you grew up and there are some people who will believe only if they see for themselves, remember Thomas who said I will not believe until I touch him, and Christ never condemn him for it contrary to what many people say. Christ is the only one who can save a soul, so don't be discourage if someone doesn't want to be saved; just do your part (one plants, the other waters, and God gives the increase) and let the Christ do the rest through the power of the Holy Spirit. Except God build a house we labor in vain.

CHAPTER 3

WHISPERS IN THE WIND

GROWING UP IN THE SOUTH I learned to enjoy the simple things in life like a quiet walk through the woods, or just sitting by a stream listening and watching the water transform the landscape, it doesn't happen all at once but a little at a time. No matter what some people think about the south you can't find a more positive and relaxing place anywhere else in the word. In Tennessee people travel for miles to watch the leaves change, sounds weird right, but if you've ever sat on a mountain in Tennessee and enjoyed the scenery you'll never forget it, the calming effect of the colors as the sun seems to dance off of the leaves, the gentle breeze, it a sight to behold. In the south, it feels like everything moves at its own pace, and on a windy day you can almost hear the wind calling your name. But later in life I found myself moving to the city and found it's easy to get engulfed in your everyday life, the constant rush, rush and the constant going from place to place, it seems like everyone is in hurry to go nowhere. Seeing all the people overly stressed, constantly competing in a dog eat dog society, makes me nostalgic for the long walks, peace, and quiet of the country life. I recall hearing a fable as a child that said, if you pick a dandelion and blow on it, the wind would carry it to the one you love. Can you imagine how many dandelions where picked as a child, when you fall in and out of love every week, we never realized it at the time but an innocent act was actually causing the dandelion to spread it seeds into fertile ground, all because of a simple wives tale. In so many churches, rumors and gossip are spread without any truth whatsoever many because of what someone else feels or believe that God has given them a special word that and they're the only person who can receive deliver it. Like the dandelion people continue to spread rumors and accusations based on hearsay without any further thought of what's going to happen to the other person. In addition, because of it the love of many is beginning to wax cold.

One of the most destructive forces in the church are the whispers in the wind, the word of God teaches us the tongue no man can tame. Let us be honest how many whispers have you heard in your church, maybe from a pastor or another lay member, the funny thing about it is that you never really see it coming, you may watch the effects of a breeze as it moves the leaves and debris but have you ever noticed that there is always an adverse effect whether bad or good? Like the natural wind there are winds in every church with a positive or negative effect, the results aren't always clear, but one thing is an absolute, that it does bring with it debris, that are scattered around from place to place. Anytime a rumor or gossip is spread inside the church, it has a devastating effect on someone, the results aren't always visible but they will appear if the form of resentment, anger, fear, jealousy, pride, envy, backbiting, and some will fall away from the church if not properly resolved. In cases like these you need an outsider someone who is not directly connected with your church or ministry someone with a spiritual and caring heart for the children of God. The word of God calls them peacemakers, if someone should era, we as children of god should restore them in a spirit of humility and meekness.

When we hear whispers, we must try to resolve them, but the strange thing about a whisper in the wind is that no one really wants to admit where they heard the rumor or how the heard it. I've learned over the years if you're tired of hearing gossip just tell people you don't want to hear it and they will generally respect that and shut up. IF you pay attention to them (like a tornado) they can warn you of impending dangers, it is up to the lay members to access the damage that may be caused by the winds if allowed to continue.

Whispers can come in many forms the most notable one is a lie, I always said there's a little truth in every lie told, and you may be thinking what do you mean? If you study the word of god and read when Jesus was on the mount fasting for forty days and nights, Satan came and tempted him. In every statement, there was a little truth, Example he said if you're the son of god turn this stone into bread, Jesus could have, but he said man shall not live by bread alone but by every word that proceed out of the mouth of God. Do you remember him asking Jesus to jump from the mountain to prove that the angels would save and protect him, but Jesus said thou shalt not tempt the Lord thy God? I'm not trying to quote every scripture that should be done at your local place of worship; but what I am trying to do is show you that Satan uses a little truth to create a big lie. I remember a young minister in a local church who loved God and wanted to see souls saved, in fact, he was very charismatic, and wow could he preach to be so young. His goal was to get people to the church so they could be saved, one Sunday he brought a nice looking female to church with him, he had been witnessing to her for quite some time trying to win her for Christ. After weeks of talking about Christ, he finally won her trust, she came, and the service was beautiful that day until the end. The pastor of that church thought it was his duty to question her in front of the whole congregation, she was questioned almost to the point of interrogation, how humiliated she must have felt to be questioned and treated like a fornicator. She never came back to that church again, and it was a long time before he brought another female to that church. As I stated earlier being in leadership you are privilege to a lot of information, some things should never be said or done. The pastor later stated that the young woman only wanted him, and they could see it all over her. I often wonder if she understood, what Christ meant when he said let the wheat grow with the tares. I wonder did anyone realized that no one joined that church for a long time after that incident, many leaders today are running ministries from day to day, waiting to hear from God on how and what should be done in today's service, afraid to move forward because of fear of offending God. Some simply wait on a touch, which may include a jerking of the limbs or movement of some other body part. They will sing for hours at a time waiting for a specific move of God, sometimes anticipating when the leader command them to shout, they shout, when commanded to sing they sing, when commanded cry they cry. It almost gives you the impression of a Simon says game. Many churches today exercise the gift of prophecy; over any other gift given, it seems as if many are searching for that heavenly anointed prophet someone who has a word from God, as if to get a new revelation. If you chase after prophesy or prophet waiting on the lord to tell you something new, you're wasting your time.

The lord has given you his word, use it, study it, and live it, allow me to back track for a moment I'm not saying there aren't any true prophets, but what I am saying is stop running to them for an answer or for prayer when you have the most high priest which is Jesus Christ, who said that once you receive the holy ghost no man need to teach you, not only that but he will guide you and comfort you. So if you want a word from God develop a relationship with him, and if you do chase anyone with a gift chose someone who has the most important gift, which is the gift of love, it will never fail you, and it's not puffed up and doesn't seek its own. Study the scripture and you'll find that one-day tongues will fail, prophecy will fail, healing will fail but love is eternal and it's the only eternal gift given to men to give freely to others. Maybe we missed the obvious and simple things God does or doesn't do in the church. I follow scripture with a lot of common sense, many things done are based on emotionalism, traditions, methods, modes, and means that we have followed because someone who couldn't rightly divide the word of truth. One thing I enjoy about Gods word is it was left open to interpretation, you see God doesn't change, it's our understanding of him and his will that constantly changes from generation to generation. In the future if you see any trash, broken pieces in the church pick it up and stop the spread of useless garbage.

CHAPTER 4

THE COURTSHIP

REMEMBER WHEN YOU WERE YOUNG in a time of innocents, do you remember your first courtship or date as we say today. Wasn't it the most exciting time in your life, you meet that special someone and your heart races with anticipation, your mind drifting into a fantasy of could this be the person I'm going to marry, could this be the person I'm going to live with for the rest of my life. At the time it seems and felt as if nothing else was equally important, you live in that moment in time without any reservations.

Especially to a teenager whose hormones are out of control, amazingly at this time in their life they focus all their energy into this person, not fully understanding the chemical changes that occur during this very sensitive time in life. I know we are not animals, but I found some astonishing similarities an example (young elephants are very dangerous when they come in musk, they're highly aggressive attacking anyone or any other animal that comes near them. But if you introduce a larger older male into a herd of young bachelor the youngster will stop becoming prematurely aggressive, even the musk cycle will begin to slow down and, in some cases, completely stop. Today we don't have many older people willing to teach the younger men and women, I remember when I was younger the older people use to say, yall don't know how to properly court, they would ask you where is the woman your courting and why haven't I meet her yet. Back then I didn't understand the importance of my elders wisdom and knowledge , it seemed as if they knew the person better than you did, they would say things like; she's no good and later in life I found out they were right, but being young you really don't want to hear that at the time because you in love, and believe you can overcome anything. As you get older, you look back on your youth and realize how stupid it all sounded. Love is really one of the greatest forces you will ever know. I know that the love of God is the greatest gift to man, but even God demanded that there be a sacrifice; so, he gave his only begotten as an atonement for our sins. God loved us so much he was willing to die for us; he dated us for hundreds if not thousands of years, even though we sinned against him again and again but yet he loved us even when we cheated on him with other Gods. When we wanted a divorce and to live our own lives, they way we saw fit, he remained faithful. Like an angry lover we submitted our divorce decree to the world court and pleaded our cause for freedom. As the bill of divorce sat on the world's desk waiting to be affirmed by our conscious and signed by humanity, we live as if he never existed. He already knows we are looking for something that he can only give which is love, peace, fulfillment of life and the realization of oneself. When we find there is nothing but emptiness in this life and we long for something or someone greater than ourselves, it is then we realize what a mistake we have made. We wonder is it too late, have my divorce papers been signed by the judge? We pick up the phone called prayer and ask the one we rejected, is it too late to work it out. Only to find him asking us where the bill of divorcement, even though we thought he divorced us he never did, he just separated himself from our sins he never divorced us. Now that's love, the ironic part of this is some things in the natural mimic some things in the spiritual. Have you ever been to a church you weren't brought up in, if you have you can understand that you never really join the first church you go too, it's like a courtship, from the outside everything seems nice at first, the church is very organized, the members appear to be one big happy family; that is until you join then it all comes out what you thought was the house of God is now the house of confusion. You begin to notice that some people don't like others and some sermons preached over the pulpit aren't from God, you find they are more hearsay and private conversations being revealed to the members of the church, leaving many wounded, torn and spiritually exhausted. Just when you thought you knew, the church, pastor, people, now your left feeling why am I here and how did I make this mistake; asking God what to do and how do I get out of this mess. It feels like a bad break up, where you don't want to offend anyone or hurt anyone's feelings after all they're your new family. Many want to get out but don't know how, others have people in their ear telling them, we need you, were glad you're here, you're so important to the ministry. Essentially you have dated the ministry, helped it to grow and now that you've seen the other side it hurts so much and you're afraid to trust, or give your heart, and spiritual growth to another ministry. The saddest part about it is some may never trust again; they feel used and abused by the church. If you think your alone, allow me to ease your pain, you're not alone, this has happened time and time again, for hundreds of years, you're not the first and you want be the last. In spite of how many men hurt you God will never hurt on purpose or for pleasure, you must remember that everyone who say they are from God they aren't. I want you to understand that God isn't in every church; the nature of men is when things go bad we want to blame him for everything, we quickly forget that the Satan has demons and some live in people; there are also those who do his will willingly. The bible teaches us that the devil walks about as a roaring lion seeking out whom he may devour; you must remember we wrestle not against flesh and blood but against principalities and spiritual wickedness in high places. One of the most important lessons Jesus taught his disciples was how to pray he taught them to cultivate a relationship with God.

Today many Christians aren't serving church, rather serving the God (Leadership) of the church, the lord said that he was seeking such to worship him in spirit and in truth; some forget the building isn't the church, the pastor isn't God. I learned what he meant when God said cursed is every man that trust in the arm of flesh, Jesus never told you trust men, only him. No matter where you go or what denomination you're in, you can't be saved by it; neither does it guarantee you a place in heaven. You are saved by grace, by faith, salvation doesn't consist of people you follow or the place of worship, but your relationship with God through Jesus Christ. The apostle Paul said who or what should separate me from the love of God.

CHAPTER 5

THE STALKER

THE BIBLE TEACHES US THAT the devil walks about as a roaring lion seeking out whom he may devour. Like the devil a lion is one of the world's top predators, he's silent when stalking his prey, he doesn't make any noise, and you can't even hear a twig break. His success usually depends on his stealth and number of other involved in the hunt. Like the lion the devils time is very short, before a bigger and more powerful person come to reclaim this world, the person of Jesus Christ.

The redeemer of the world, I believe when he returns it will not be something that's subtle or quiet thing that some people will miss it or didn't notice it. I believe that when he returns the entire world will know it at once. I believe when the king of kings and lord of lord returns the adversary will have to retreat like a lion when he sees a bigger and more powerful lion coming, he retreats or die in battle. One thing that causes many people to become apostates is the reality that, there are some bad people in the church. Believe it or not Christ hasn't returned to deal with some of mess that goes on inside the four walls; some wonder how a loving, and all-powerful God could allow this to go on in his house. Many churches today are opportunist they look for someone who is profitable to their ministry or someone who doesn't have many if any issues to deal with. In some case they look for the doctors, lawyers, bankers, realtors, minister or lay members who were profitable to their former churches. It sounds unreal, but it really happens today in some of the world's largest ministries' and some of the smaller ones. Some are looking for financial gain while other are looking for that spiritual gain, someone who has gifts, someone who's marketable to the masses of people. I'm reminded of young married couple who had two children and had fallen upon some financial difficulty to the point that they lost their house to the bank and had to relocate to another state. Mrs. Williams had just receive a job with her new employer before they move and her employer was a pastor of small church, the church was larger than any that Mr. and Mrs. Williams had ever attended. They seemed to have a thriving ministry, with a daycare business, travel bus, after school program, and couple rental properties. The pastor question them about their former church and what jobs they did in the church and what they could bring to the ministry, after hearing their story of being raped and abused by their former pastor, this pastor assured them it will never happen to them hear; in fact she gave her a job making twice what she once made, and gave them a place to stay at a reasonable price, it was an offer they couldn't pass up. They immediately move to their newfound blessing and received much praise from the members of the ministry and move into very important positions in the church with in one or two weeks of attending without any restrictions which made them somewhat suspicious. When they move into the house, they were promised it had a few unknown problems, there was no hot water or heat in the middle of winter the pastor assured them she would take care of it, and never did, they took cold showers. They made what little heat they could in the fireplace, because it's very hard to find wood in the city and if you do it's very expensive, did I mention they had to pay the previous tenants electric bill who by chance happen to be the pastors daughter. They stayed believing that Mrs. Williams would be paid what she was promised, and they could get back on their feet. Needless to say, that the job the pastor promised was a minimum wage job, the job was a lie, and even more harmful she endure listening to pastor curse and yell at her members on a daily basis. As long as the church was growing from the contributions Mr. & Mrs. Williams brought to it everyone believes the church was alright, new people began coming to the church and praise and worship changed from boring to spiritual and effective.

After a short time, Mrs. Williams began working more hours for less pay, the church had scheduled programs for members, when you finished working you had to be there. Participating in some program or function that's how it was six days a week, and if you didn't attend you were called and reprimanded on the phone for not being committed to the ministry, they rarely if ever had any time for each other or their children, within a short time they burned out on going to church and the pastor began making life more and more difficult. The pastor wanted to increase their responsibility and even offered to give Mr. Williams a second job to make ends meet, Mr. Williams explained to me he couldn't make ends meet because they never received the pay, she promised. Mrs. Williams soon suffered a small heart attack and the pastor wanted her rent now without any excuses and you better pay your tithes. Needless to say, they left that ministry and house after a few months for a better apartment with electric and heat it was larger in size for less rent. The scars that were left on their hearts will forever be a reminder that everyone who says they're of God really isn't. I'm sad to say that ministry still exist today and is functioning as if nothing ever happened. To this day their biggest regret is not the awful conditions they endured being lied too, deceived, humiliated or use, but it's the souls that came to that ministry because of what they were doing there and the many people where and are currently manipulated and don't have the strength to leave. We love to talk about sowing seed on good ground, but we rarely talk about what Jesus meant when he said let the wheat grow with the tares. I believe that God allows us to go through some experiences to make us stronger, wiser, smarter, and more aware of what's going on in the world today.

CHAPTER 6

THE ATTACK

LOOK OUT IS A PHRASE we all are familiar with, if you heard it, you knew some impending danger is on the way. It's a shame we can't say that about most churches and sound the alarm before people get involved in a bad church experience; like many churches the rapist or attacker watch their victims for a period before assaulting them. It is a rare event when a rape is by chance; or an uncalculated event. You may be wonder what do you mean, I often think about how many people would be attacked if they wore a police uniform or were very muscular, very few, I think? A rapist is like a cowardly coyote who seeks any opportunity to feed himself with the least amount of effort, some seek prey they can easily overpower that want cause much of a struggle or a big commotion. Like the coyote, there are people in the church who seek the spiritually weak and wounded the object is to overpower and inflict a great amount of fear in the victim so that they won't fight or cry out for help.

There are many victims in the world today who have been broken by the rules and the doctrines of men rather than the word of God. The majority of the time it goes unreported, or unnoticed. Some even think it's not my problem, their ok, my pastor wouldn't ever hurt anyone, they think this way because it's not there wife, daughter, future wife, who you marry and later find they have some unresolved issues with members in the church; It can become difficult for them to reach their full potential until they have been healed by Jesus Christ he came to heal the broken heart and set the captives free.

Let me emphasize this again most attacks occur by someone you know or have met. To help you understand what I'm talking about, I want to tell you a story about a young lady named Sandy.

Here's her story, I was walking home one night after attending a church service it began to rain, but I didn't have enough money for bus fare, I was too afraid to hitch hike; in the city that can be very dangerous for a young lady(as you'll see most victims are oblivious to their attackers schemes). I heard a horn behind me, and I looked to see who it was, to my surprise It was a young pastor from another church whom she had visited before. Sandy said, I thought what a blessing, as I got into the car, he notice I was soaked, but didn't say much about it, he said I have to stop by my place for a moment to pick up something before I take you home. When we arrived at his place, he invited me upstairs to see his new keyboard he had for the church, he knew I loved music, because I play the keyboard at my church. When we enter his apartment he locked his door behind us, which at the time really wasn't strange at the time, he walked to his bedroom while I stood there admiring all of the new equipment he purchased and I didn't want to get any of his furniture wet. He later returned with a long t-shirt and said put this on while I dry your clothes and then I'll take you home; it kind of bothered me at first but he's a pastor a man of God I can trust him. So I changed into the t-shirt because that's all he gave me then he took all of my clothes to the dryer, I could sit down now and he sat beside me, our conversation started out normal but then he began telling me how beautiful I was and he touched me, I immediately felt uncomfortable and demanded that he take me home, he said walk home in the rain and I realized I was further away from home than when I started, knowing I had no other way home I didn't fight him as he forced himself upon me. The worst part was the after, when he wanted me to play the keyboard while so he could practice his homiletics and preaching. Every time I saw him after that day it made my stomach turn, I felt sick and dirty, if this story is hard to hear you better believe it was even harder for sandy to tell, she wanted to be free from years of carrying the shame, hurt, and betrayal.

I wonder if the tables had been turned what would he have done or how would he have reacted. After hearing countless stories like Sandy's it hard not to lose faith in leadership and the church, it makes one wonder who is real and who can you trust, after hearing what seem like the same story form different people, I must admit my faith was shaken little by little with every heartbreaking story. But I survived with the help of writers such as (T.D Jakes, Phillip Yancy, Ravi Zach, G.K Chesterton, Max Lucado, only to name a few). These men help me to see that we must focus our eyes on the person of Christ who is the only perfect person who will never leave you nor forsake you. As the apostle Paul stated follow me while I follow Christ, so if he should stray, we still have our goal in sight which is to have fellowship with a loving and forgiving God.

Jesus said that offense must come, but woe unto the man that they come through.

CHAPTER 7

SOLITUDE

SOLITUDE A WORD THAT CAN either be a blessing or curse, there are some people who pray for it and others who pray not to have, it all depends on your perspective and the circumstances that surround your life. There are times in our life were some hurts and pain seem to out weight others, like breaking and arm or a leg: or losing someone close to you. Suddenly, as you read in the previous chapters the physical pain is far easier to get over than the mental pain that can sometime go on for years and years, without proper counseling or a strong support system, in your life most people never recover. I have learned to apply the scriptures to everyday life, one of my favorites is (weeping may endure for a night, but joy comes in the morning). I've learned that some days will be night, and the night seems to outlast the day, but without it I wouldn't be able to enjoy the day or cultivate a closer relationship with my heavenly father. I learn in the darkness of night it's easier to hear God speak because there are less distractions in my heart, mind, and my ears are attentive to his voice. Yes, I understand how it feels when your nights last for days, months and even some time years. You know how it feels not to have food, or gas, even a place to stay in those circumstances it hard to wait for the day when the wicked seem to be prospering. Most people when they're having had time seem to isolate themselves from other because of embarrassment or they don't want to feel humiliated by others that seem to want to give a stern pep talk and a lot of useless advice about your personal finances when you don't even have any to invest.

Please don't be embarrassed about not having money like some of the great television pastors or bishops, some of them didn't obtain wealth overnight, and many of them struggled for many years, in the same situations you and I face today.

I want you to know that even at your worst there is always someone who is willing to trade place with you in your worst moments, from the homeless man living under a bridge in Newark NJ in the winter, to a new mother who just found out she has only a year to live. To the father who has to face his hungry children, to the wife who is in prison for the rest of her life, you my friend are not alone. I'm sure that somewhere in America there's someone sitting in a church who will be kicked out of their house in a few days, or someone who's believing God to pay their bills only to be disappointed. In time like these that's when God is the closest to us, the word of God teaches us that we don't have a high priest (which can't be touched by our pain) Jesus sees and feels them all and be confident that God is going to get the glory out of this somehow, like my brother Job said (though he slay me yet will I trust him). Have you ever notice when Job was sick he was never alone, and when God created Adam he said that (it is not good that man should be alone), and God created Eve to be a partner with Adam, even God himself isn't alone so why would he leave you alone with no one to talk too or share your problems with, he is our wonderful counselor, our prince of peace if you allow him.

SUFFER THE LITTLE CHILDREN

I can't leave this chapter without talking about solitude and the way it affects those in the church who have been raped in one way or another. Solitude can effect different people in different ways but have you ever notice how a child who has been mentally or physically abused by a parent or stranger behavior changes, I'm not calming to be a doctor or psychologist but there are some tell all signs of abuse in most cases, ex. Some children tend to shy away from that person or adult, even if their not the person who abused them they shy away from what they represent, they will not talk to or make eye contact with some who they think could hurt them, some leave the room that they are in when a particular person enters, other have panic attacks and run refusing to talk to anyone until they feel it is safe to do so and today we have many adults who haven't dealt with childhood issue that are still haunting them. More and more we are seeing children and adults coming forward saying how they were molested and raped physically by a priest, uncle, family member, or stranger. I think the past ten years has been a real eye opener for most American who think they are safe where ever they go, it's sad to say most people think of rape they think of it as a male or female crime or a man attacking a child, rarely do we think of a women who sexually assault boys or little girls, it's a startling fact that women molest children just like men, and finally we are begging to see male as victims too, allow me to ask you a question how many time in the news have you seen a female teacher having sex with a child under age from elementary to middle school to many times I bet. In our society, females seem to get lighter or no prison time for their crimes against children as unfair as it is men get tougher sentences, I refuse to take sides for either, but the crimes should be treated the same for male and female because the effects are the same, both victim seem to withdraw from society or end up in trouble with the law because of past issues they haven't resolved. Rape occurs in every culture in the world also in every religion, if your Baptist, Methodist, Catholic, Universals, Holiness, Jew wake up its happening. There are many books out there that would explain why they do what they do from early childhood development to anger with their parents I'm not trying to debate there studies of human behavior, what I have a problem with is telling the victim of rape (oh they just suffer from low self-esteem, or their trying to regain some love that's missing in their early development as a child, he was just asserting his authority over you don't resist and he will stop or lose a desire for you. As a lay member I see the same thing happening in churches today, as members try to protect pastors who yell and scream at others because they can and they don't have any one to answer to, so they feel they can do whatever they want.

I've seen people submit to leadership every demand only to be humiliated in front of the congregation for not raising enough money, or not being on time or singing in the right key in choir, without anyone to come to their defense many isolate themselves from the church others sit in the corner and remain a victim for years and years, facing the one who hurt them every Sunday. Without proper counseling they will remain in a state of stagnation never to reach their full potential in Christ. If you have experience any of this, you're not alone neither are meant to be alone. The lord said cast all your cares on him for he cares for you, and to take up your cross daily and follow him. If your currently in a church where your being abuse, I advise you to pray about, it may be time to leave if it keeps the peace. Remember it was never the mission of Jesus to abuses the people in any way, it was his mission to redeem, restore, help and heal the people.

CHAPTER 8

ANGER

ANGER IS A FEELING THAT we all understand, yet each and every one of us deal with it different. We get angry when someone cuts us of on the road, or if were insulted by them with a gesture or in speech it all brings a form of anger, but today I would like to direct your attention to the type of anger that many experience when they are rape in the church. Let me begin by saying that rape is a horrible thing committed by some of the sickest people, it's an offense against the body, mind and soul: the attacker violates the very nature of the victim without any remorse at the time or any consideration of the long term effect it's going to have on them or their family. While talking to many victims there are some common themes that must be addressed the feeling of filthy, solitude, I deserved this, anger, rationalize, the feeling of what did I do wrong, or what did I do to deserve this, it will never happen to me just to name a few. But anger out of all the feelings can be one of the most destructive of them all. When someone is angry it can be harmful for the victim, their family, and the attacker. The victim can easily become the victimizer for many generations if there not careful or haven't worked through the whole process of healing, in this section one particular person comes to mind let's call him Timothy. Timothy was once raped in the church and thought he had resolved all his old issues, he believed he was fine and everything would be alright the thought he was strong enough to heal himself and for many years he went about his everyday life like nothing ever happened and he began to conduct ministry in other churches until he began attending a new church and a lot of things he had out grown or learn differently was to begin to manifest in the new church.

He tried to warn the pastor about the upcoming storm, because he had seen it all before to him it was like watching a bad movie again and again and there was nothing he could do about it he said to himself I've talked to the pastor of the church I can't supersede there authority besides it's not my church I'm here to learn and be taught of the lord. Like Timothy many of us just brush things aside and say were putting it in Gods hands, which is not always scripturally sound or wise. Timothy confessed how much, he really believes in the pastor of that church, and if fasted and prayed it would be handled. All too often like timothy many of us think if we just pray about it, it will all be worked out by god through his leaders, needless to say timothy was disappointed to see the members of that church leave, because like timothy they saw the same things fornication, adultery, favoritism, and the pastor exalt the most flamboyant preacher the one who had a word or prophesy from God. Timothy thought I must go away on a business trip for a few weeks I'll leave the men's ministry in their hands, they'll be ok. After talking with the pastor and assistant pastor, he left for a few weeks only to realize that while he was gone no one ever called or inquired about how he was doing the men that he mentor never once call not even the pastor. He was devastated, the same men he was teaching appeared like they never learn anything, or did they fall for the tricks or charisma of another. Needless to say, Timothy's time was limited there after that event he showed up less and less at church and he usually sat in the front of the church now he sat in the back, the same place he sat when he first came to that church. Sometime people are on their way out of the door, but we seldom recognize it. Maybe because we think they are strong and can handle anything, or we don't notice they are hurting, when someone is hurting in a place where they feel they have no voice or aren't being heard they tend to leave silently as they came. My thoughts turn to what if someone would have noticed a change in his behavior, or notice how every Sunday he seems to move further away from the alter an pulpit. The pulpit is something that a member should seek to get closer too, because of the spoken word of god ministering to the people; it should draw us closer to God and not push us away from him. I'm not at all advocating the way that timothy left that church, I believe it was wrong and I pray one day he revisit the decision he made by leaving without talking to leadership or explaining how he felt. It was more of his past that caused him to leave than anything that they ever did too him, he never let go of his past hurts and disappointments before joining another ministry. Be sure you have resolved all your past issues or seek help in the resolution of them before you commit yourself to any ministry, if not you could become more toxic or harm than productive to a church. The gift that God has given you is for the edification of the body of Christ, it's not intended to cause division or discord in the church but to draw the member of the body together in the bonds of love. Anything that does the opposite is not of God, even when God allowed Israel to go into captivity again and again, he did it because he love them and wanted their hearts to turn towards him. He only wanted to have fellowship with them and protect them from the things in the world, an even though they turned their back on him again and again he made a provision for all men in the distant future for them to be redeemed. That's true ministry and true love, will you take a lesson from God today and make a provision for someone else today.

DISGRACED & REJECTED

Recently I was talking to a woman, who told me of her experiences involving church hurt. For the purpose of this book we shall call her Faith. If anyone ever had a normal life, you would think it was faith, she was brought up in a very religious house hold, with a very strict mother and no father in the home. She was the perfect example of what a kind gentle Christian should be in every aspect of their life.

Faith was a quiet and gently woman, she never seemed to get angry with anyone for any reason. If someone hurt her or offended her, she would just find a place to quietly cry, never wishing any ill thing to happen to them. She was the type of woman who would help the person that just took advantage of her in the worst way. I could help but think how any man could seek to hurt a great woman. I'm not in any way suggesting that Faith is innocent or hasn't ever done anything wrong in her life, but the more I listen to her the more question began to arise in my mind. Faith is single mother with two teenage boys, whom I have met and have great respect for. She raised them without spanking them, or having to yell at them that much, to listen to her speak I wonder if it was possible for her too yell or scream at all. Some would even say it's impossible for a woman to raise a male child without them getting into trouble or hanging out in the streets, her sons enjoys the presence of their mother, and like her would give their last to help anyone in need. Her voice is very soft and quiet it's a non-threating voice in every sense of the word. Many times, she told me of guys who made advance toward her and she told them no, but I never stopped their advances, some time to the point where she would be pinned in a corner with no way out crying. Faith wasn't like anyone I have ever met she doesn't have a will to fight or harm anyone, some doctors would say it's from her being abuse by men, which I would have to disagree. I asked faith had she ever been abuse as a child or molested her answer was no, I thought it would be possible to catch her in my next question, (have you ever hurt any animals or insects as a child). Faith said no, that would be wrong. I would not have believed it if I didn't witness her on more than one occasion fan a mosquito or dog fly who just bit her away with her hand. My question was why you didn't kill it. She always said the same thing a (that would be wrong). So, it surprises me greatly when faith began to share her stories of church hurt. I told her of this book I was writing, and she could identify with a few of the people in it. With her permission I asked if I could share her story with you but be warned it may shock you.

Faith was very religious home as I told you earlier, after graduating high school faith had a child without being married. Being from a very spiritual family she was a disgrace to the family and to the church. She was told she would never be anything or accomplish anything in life, that she just ruined her life, and her kids would be thugs in the streets, no man would ever want to marry her especially with children. Her mother decided before the first child was born that Faith need to apologize to the church for disgracing the church and her family. One Sunday Unknown to her faiths' mother spoke to the pastor and informed him that her daughter was pregnant with a child. After the service was over the pastor call Faith to the front of the church sat her in a chair and began scolding her in front of the church, how wrong she was, and how big of a sin it was in Gods sight. What hit me the hardest was when she said her pastor stated (she better hope God will forgive her for this) many in the pews agreeing with the pastor as faith just sat there and cried? She said she really didn't want to go up front, but everyone knew who the pastor was calling or talking about, she decide it's better to get it over with now. Just as I thought I heard the worst of it, she shocked me with another revelation. As a part of her punishment for disgracing the church she would lecture the teens in the church every Sunday about how wrong it was to have premarital sex, she did this every Sunday without fighting or complaining. I was thinking surely that's the end, but no there was more, as a part of her punishment she would watch the children and toddlers of the church every Sunday. I asked Faith how long this punishment last, did it last until you had your first child, she said no. it lasted for the next ten years or so. I couldn't help but be intrigued by the time that passed, so I asked her did anyone else ever have a child out of wed-lock, in the church during that time, she said yes but I was still stuck keeping everyone else's children in the church while service went on without me. I could hardly believe what I was hearing for years you missed service at your own church as a punishment, something you did ten years ago.

I'm always amazed at how, men try to take the place of God and pronounce the judgments of God on someone they disagree with or someone has hurt their feelings and send them to hell in their own minds or idea of what God is going to do. Many lay members forget that God sent his only son to redeem us at the time that we deserved it the least, God chose to execute his divine justice on himself in the person of Jesus because he could not allow any sin to go unpunished. Even though he didn't do anything to deserve this punishment he accepted for us. Wow what an awesome God we serve, how many of us know of someone who would willingly take the death penalty for a crime we committed, that's what God did for you and for me.

Faith understood this more than many Christians who go to church and sit in the pews every Sunday, I will be the first to admit I would not have gone through all of that, but she did and still wanted to go to church and learn more about God, she still carries a hunger and thirst for the word and a relationship with God. She never blamed anyone for her failures except herself, if I had to guess I think her being around so many little children kept her innocent to what was going on in the church and how the church functions. Over the years I have observed that children have a way of making the toughest and biggest adult surrender to a baby or very young child. We in some senses revert to a state of youthfulness, connecting with them in ways we could never connect with another adult. When I see faith from time to time, she always reminds me of God's grace, how she is always willing to give to other even though she doesn't have anything to give. How is that someone who knows so little about God can mirror his love so perfectly and those who worship in the church building do such a good job of mirroring the devil. I know it sounds tough but remember Satan was once an angel in heaven, he was in a perfect place and God trusted him with much. Until he said ill exalt my throne above the stars, how many of us step out of a place that God has position us just to achieve some notoriety or prestige. Jesus gave his life, for you and for me that we may take up the cross and follow him daily, he was betrayed, whip, lied to, and abandon by the ones that he loved. He was even mocked and scorned on the cross, but he never fought back or made one threat toward humanity for what they were doing to him. The bible teaches us he was led like a sheep to the slaughter, yet he opened not his mouth. Every time I read and think about what he did I think it took strength, character, determination, purpose, and humility just to name a few. He was the person I strive to be like every day, but I'm a constant work in progress. Yet there are those like faith who haven't been tainted by inner workings of the church and is always willing and ready to be sacrificed for the cause of Christ. To me faith is an inspiration, she shows love to everyone, but they never see her more than an average person. As a church we need to get back to basic and lose all pride, positions and titles, and become the servants that Jesus was to all men. What is our purpose on this earth but to love, server, glorify, win souls for him? Faith has taught me, even though others in the church abuse you and put you down every day in the name of Christianity, that none of us are perfect, but God still loves you. It's not what they say or do to me, but it's what I do too them in the name of Jesus Christ. I must exemplify Christ in everything I do and say regardless of what is going on around me, God is still in control, and judgment belongs only to God, he is the one who will judge us in the last days not men according to every work that's done in this flesh. Today make a decision and seek to please God in all your ways.

CHAPTER 9

NO EXCLUSIONS

SOME MAY THINK THAT JUST because you serve and trust god, that you're exempt from pain and heartache. I learned when I was a young minister that was far from the truth, I learned the more you grow in grace the more you will experience in life. I've learned that some things will break down yourself will, so you can have a better and stronger relationship with God. I also learned that the people you love and trust the most are the one the devil can and will use to hurt you the deepest. This fact was brought back to my memory when I was talking to a very close friend of mine, for the purpose of this book we will call him Thomas. Thomas was a minster in his thirty's who had lost his church due to differences in vision an opinion, he didn't attend any other church regularly if any at all. For Thomas it was like a slow and painful death to hear someone else minister Gods word, he could never hear what they were saying unless they had a heavy anointing on them. It wasn't that he did not want to hear what was said, but his mind would drift, and he would be delivering his own sermon inside of his on head. Thomas gave me glimpse of his hurt when he told me how he lost his wife, to another man or so-called prophet of God. Thomas is the typical American man who, worked most of his life to support his family, he had two stepchildren who he love and one child of his own. Thomas was dedicated to the church, family, job, he would always say faith first, fact second and my feelings last. Thomas was wounded in many churches, following his wife trying to please her and god, (notice the order) he left many churches trying to keep the peace. One day after twelve years of marriage Thomas, told his wife he couldn't fight to save their marriage any more. He explained how he felt for years being beaten down by female pastors and not doing what god wanted him to do. I must interject this, there are many great female pastors in the world today, this is just how Thomas felt at that time. Thomas shared his vision with his wife, she agrees to help bring it about with him but never did. What he did not know at the time was she had a hidden motivation. It was the honor of being a first lady without putting in any real work. Needless to say, the ministry didn't last very long. The very ones Thomas thought were for him was plotting against him in the church. After deciding to leave, he decided to take a year sabbatical, he talked to people about god, when and where he could, but his focus was on taking care of his family and job. His wife came to him on more than one occasion saying how she wanted him in church, and she could no longer take being alone in church. She was so tired of making excuses for why Thomas was not at church every Sunday or why he chose to stay home today. Thomas didn't care what people thought of him anymore, he had been abused by church folks for over a decade, he wanted to stay away and get himself together. Thomas decided to go to school and earn his college degree like his wife did, he supported her for ten years as she earned her degree, so now it was his turn the kids were grow except one and out of the house sometimes on their own. He thought he could get the same support that he had shown her for so many years, instead after attending two classes, his wife became very jealous of the new friends he made at school and all the group meetings he attended. She began making accusations that Thomas was cheating with other women, and "why did they have to have so many meetings", when in reality it was only once a week. He assured her nothing was happening allowed her to listen to his conversations always told her where and when the meetings were. It never helped or stopped the accusations. One day, Thomas notices that his wife had been talking with a few old high school friends for some time but wanted to trust her with anything or anyone. Later he discovered that a few of them had serious feelings for her and he warned her about them, she at first denied it and later admitted to one of them having feeling for her besides he lived over twelve hrs.' away so nothing could ever happen. Thomas confessed the marriage had been on the rocks for some years now, but he wanted to trust God that everything was going to work out.

WOLF IN MY OWN HOUSE

I really don't want to leave everyone in suspense as to what happen to Thomas, but if I did this book would be incomplete. Thomas said later that his heart had been broken many times by the woman he said he loved, without her ever acknowledging she was wrong about any argument. He always made excuses in his head for her behavior, it was stress from school, the kids, or the church business, what every sounded good or rational in his head. Maybe it was the little amount of money he made and paying the mortgage, car note, a vacuum cleaner bill, alarm systems, clothes for the kids, regular utilities, and gas which made her angry because at the end of the month there was never any money. He said "I did my best" but it never seems to be enough for his wife, she always compared their lives to what the jones had, what other relatives had, or other friends had. I almost forgot to ask Thomas to finish talking about the old friend she had on the internet. Thomas sat back with a very focus intense stare looking at the ceiling. He said well, she said that she had a revival to preach at a church up north, but she never told him where, just up north at the beginning of the year. By this time the marriage was already over, they had already agreed to wait until the middle of year to file for a divorce; they had divided all the assets and agree to be civil with each other. A few months later things took a turn for the worse, she told Thomas that she no longer lives at their residence, and she wasn't responsible for any of the bills. She also informed him that she wanted alimony because she could not work, because of her disability. Thomas said I help her get her master's degree for the past ten years and disability in the last two years and now she does want to use that degree that's crazy. She never worked for 4 months straight for twelve years; she always quit her jobs saying she couldn't go to school and work at the same time. Now that it's my time to go to school and I work she wanted alimony, he said no (banging his fist on the table). Thomas said she bounced in and out of his house for months sometimes sleeping on the couch, he explained they haven't slept in the same room since the previous year. She eventually went up north to preach her revival, he sent her money for their son while they were up there, he asked "isn't the church supposed to take care of you when you're coming in from anther state", and she said they didn't have any money. She later stole money out of Thomas bank account to help finance her way back to the south. As I said earlier, they had separated everything even bank accounts, Thomas said he had a separate account set up for her to support their son. Thomas face seemed to change as he explained how he took care of her children, was adopting a child and now she's changing everything they agreed too. It's was as if a sense of disgust came over his face, he didn't appear to be the same person. Thomas took a deep sigh and said" I later found out that she went pick up her past boyfriend" the one she was online with chatting with last year. This had been going on for months if not years, and he never saw the signs or didn't care to see what was going on. Thomas said this did not hurt him because he had already dealt the idea of failed marriage, and that she was free to do whatever she wanted to do. He said he had moved on some time ago, by acknowledging the hurt, rejection, humiliation, disgrace, shame, and idea of losing his adopted son and family members. He said it took him a year prior to the divorce, too cycle through many different emotions, and those closest to him never figured out what was going on. What we need to understand is that no divorce just happens overnight; Thomas said this was in the works for years and he had been preparing himself for it. As the divorce loomed on for what seemed like forever Thomas said jokingly, he moved on as did she. She was living with her new boyfriend he was looking into dating again, both of them seem happy again now that she moved to another state. Thomas began introducing his adopted son to his new friend, but when his mother found out, everything turned again for the worse. She began to threaten Thomas that he better leave her alone, and he would never see his son again if he started dating her. Thomas said that sounded crazy, they both moved on, what's the big deal. She later sent Thomas many emails trying to convince him to come back, and fight for her. He told her it was over," they discuss that years ago, and he move on like she did. She called his family members telling them how she was going to ruin his life if he didn't come back. Thomas explained to his family how she left him and had a new life before he considered dating and he was fine with that. Thomas said she was true to her word she had him arrested on false charges, ruined his name almost lost his job and his name was forever on the internet as committing a crime. She had done this same thing to her first husband, Thomas said he later discovered this after the case against him was dismissed, but the damage had already been done. Just like the wolf, Thomas's ex-wife plotted and planned her attack, she wanted him not only isolated but tired and broken down. She had planned this for months, with experience from her previous marriage. She separated him from family and friends for years, by keeping him in her circle of family, friends, and work only. He never did or visited his family with her but always went to her family's events. Like the wolf the goal is to isolate its prey from the herd, find out where its weakness is an exploit that weakness. After many years of praying on his weakness for church, family, work, she used these things to keep him isolated and weak, she never thought that God was still in control of the courts, his job and his faith. Thomas said the whole thing was bittersweet, because if this had not happened, he would have never met the woman of his dreams. As with the story of Job the devil, took one son temporally and God gave Thomas two wonderful boys. Thomas admitted no one child can replace another, but it does help ease the pain loss. He also stated he believed that his son that was taken would one day be given back to him in Gods time. Thomas reminisces about the bond he had with his son and how they did everything together and he is a replica of Thomas which will prayerfully lead them back together.

CHAPTER 10

HIDDEN AGENDAS

MANY OF US GO THROUGH life with a sense that nothing bad will ever happen if I do what I'm supposed to do and obey the law. As a child we go through life not knowing about any laws or even caring if one existed. When we become teenagers, we learn about laws and how they are used to protected our own rights and the rights of others. But something changes when we become adults, we learn that the laws are written can protect not only our rights and the rights of other. We learn that it takes a majority to change government and laws are there for structure and protection. Imagine yourself riding in your car you obey basic traffic laws most of the time without even thinking about it. Until you get into an accident now you need those who protect and serve (the Police). You may feel a sense of loss or damage because of the accident, it is imperative that the police hear your side of the story. Why is it so important that they get it right the first time? Because of small thing that most states require every driver to have is insurance. As an adult you know the importance of keep your insurance rates down and to avoid any vehicle violations. Doesn't it seem strange that you and I pay for insurance for years never needing it until we have an accident? When the accident occurs, our premium tends to go up if we are the at fault driver. We pay for the confidence and security that no money will come out of our pocket if we are not the at fault driver. What if we took one hundred drives who paid one hundred dollars a month for insurance? That's a one hundred twenty thousand dollars a year for all of the drivers. If we take those same drivers and acknowledge at least 10 had and accident that year (nothing major) causing damages of thirty-five hundred dollars each that's a grand total of thirty-five thousand dollars a year paid out. What happens to the rest of the money? I know and understand they insurance companies must pay for hospital visits and in some cases death expenses and settlements. Its not just about banking the money even though it is a business and every business wants to make a profit for itself or its investors. Even though they provide you with a contract and as you to read over it before you sign, really how many of us ever really do that? We think its to much legal garbage and all we want to know is will we be protected if something happens as soon as we walk out of the front door. What we really don't want to read or fail to acknowledge is the fine print at the bottom of the page. How many times have you seen a commercial on television by some attorney who says he's there to help or protect you? Do you ever just turn the sound down and read the small letters try it sometimes it will really change the way you see advertisements. What about the cell phone companies who always promise they have the best coverage in the whole nation, but if you read the small print you may see its only base on a particular area, year, or independent group survey. Its not that they are misleading you, its just up to you to take the time to read the small print. I have been in many churches or ministries throughout the years and what I have found is that you must be carful because some people have hidden agendas. They will sell you what looks good on the surface and omit the fine print of what's really going on. In some churches today many have stepped away for what Jesus commanded his disciples to do that is (God into the world and preach the gospel, baptizing them in the name of the father, son, and holy spirit, and the rest will he set in order when he comes back). If we compare the church from 40 years ago and the church of today it would be shocking to most. Many years ago, we had churches today we have ministries, years ago we had devotional service today we have praise and worship. I remember having a deacon board, today we have general boards, and not all of these changes are necessarily bad things. It becomes a bad thing when we have hidden agendas in mind while making changes that will bring glory and honor to men instead of God. Its easy to be caught up in some churches today who have everything you would every want in a ministry, they have babysitting services, child care, schools, colleges, banks, housing, business loans, on tv, entertainers every month, biblical scholars, praise dance, worship classes, speaking in unknown tongues (what)? The list just goes on and on, but are you really paying attention to the fine print, are looking at what's really going on in the church. Are they a family or just pretending to be a family, are they teaching the word of God or what fits into their own perspective of what the bible is saying? Are they practicing or living the word of God without making excuses of being human and everyone makes mistakes in life? I always advise new leaders you will never know how a church really functions or is dysfunctional until you assume a position of leadership. It is then very evident that sister Susan does like sister Maria, and bother Jared is sleeping with brother hills wife and the new baby she has may not be brother hills. You learn everyone who is delivering a message on Sunday morning or teaching bible study is not always in a place spiritually to do so. They are unfit spiritually to lead the flock but are allowed to do so either because no one else will step up and challenge them or it would be an embarrassment to the ministry if the secret got out. I have seen churches keep pastors in place knowing that they have some sexual, drug, alcohol, lying, among many other issues they have not reconciled with God. Today many churches are more concerned with keeping a pastor or leader who can fill the seats of the church and make sure the bills are paid, than about the personal life of the leader. I know I have heard it before (We all make mistakes) Yes, we do "however" the bible says should a man continue in sin God forbid. We want even to discuss the parable Jesus gave about the dog going back to his own vomit. Through the years I have witness those who only preach for power and money. They enjoyed having control over others in every aspect of their lives. They controlled where they went, who they fellowshipped with, what they ate, how much they gave in the offering, where they worked, who they could be friends with. At this point its no longer a church or a ministry it has become a cult. Complete control and submission. Let me very clear there is nothing wrong with submission, when we submit to God and his will. You must remember that submission does not mean stupid or gullible. Its always important to remember when God created man and woman, he created them with free will. They were to have fellowship with him, it was his desire for them to love and obey him by choice. Who wants some one to say they love them because they have too or because you're the only thing they know? Love is not a feeling or and emotion it was demonstrated by God when he gave his son. Love is a choice, its sad to see many couples divorce and separated because they said their no longer in love. Its amazing that God said choose this day whom ye will serve. Today we see members in the church who say that they love you and some of them are truly authentic. Then there is the other side of the coin, there are those who only love what they can get out of you.

I learned there are two kinds of people those who are there for the ministry and those who are there for the pastor. Regardless of which one you encounter it should not be taken as they are bad people or have hidden agendas, what you should learn is the difference in the two which will save you from future hurt and pain. Unfortunately, those who have hidden agendas rarely see the causalities they leave behind. The goal is never to edify the body or to build someone up, the goal is self-gratification. How many times have we met someone in ministry who have children by multiple women in the church, or those who have an alternative lifestyle? Whatever that means to the individual, its become quite clear that the standards of holiness that were held by the church 40 years ago is not the same today. Many young minsters today say they are called by God to go into ministry, which I respond that's nice, but did he tell you to go now? Have you counted the cost? Many see televangelist and think if I just preach hard and sound good, I can be just like them with a mega church. To which I respond the ministry in which God has called you should never be predicated on become a mega church pastor. Have you counted the cost are you willing to become a servant to all even if know one ever knows your name?

BLINDED BY NEED

I must deviate from the previous stories and focus on something that effects many churches today, especially new and start up churches. In most inner city's if you drive down any road, you see a plethora of pop up churches as we call them. They are what seems like every corner and each has its own ministry or vision for the community. There are times when I think why so many small churches why can't they all just unite for a common purpose of glorifying God and lifting him up. If we serve the same the same God and recognize a power that is higher than us, why can't we place our petty difference aside? Now it appears if you don't do this or you don't do that you're not in the perfect will of God. I have heard this term used so many times as a young minister, please understand I'm not trying to change the way you think "however" I do want to challenge the way you perceive things. Are any of us really in the perfect will of God, are we doing everything that he commanded or required us to do? I believe God is not only forgiving and graceful he understands we are human being who are flawed since the fall of Adam, we will never be perfect until he comes back and prefect us in his own image. For many of these small churches they were started due to a need not being met, or someone believing he or she has new vision for ministry. Sometimes it's just plain jealously and division that cause a split in churches. I was riding to the Myrtle Beach one warm and beautiful summer and a church sign caught my eye for some unknown reason, I will change the name for the purpose of this book, the sign said John the Baptist, United Baptist Church (not the real name) and less than a half a mile away another church had a sign out front saying, The Original John the Baptist, United Baptist Church. I was so blown away by the churches with the same title only a feet hundred yards away. I wonder what happened to make them split and yet have the same name, was there a scandal, did someone have a difference in opinion, or was it a money issue, whatever the cause I know it had to be huge due to the close proximity of both buildings? As a young minister I learn quickly about what bills needed to be paid in the church and how hard it was to raise the funds to cover every bill. Small churches usually don't have the support of those in political and financial power in the community, when you have a start up church that what it means your on your own in every way. There are those who prey on small churches and seek to exploit their need for funds and encouragement, they see them as vulnerable sheep ready to be taken in by those famous words "The Lord Said". I knew a young pastor named Robert who had taken on a start up church believing that God would somehow make away for his church to exist if he just kept the faith and kept the doors open. Robert was very optimistic that God could use him anywhere at anytime without any reservation. Robert quickly found out that with leadership comes a great responsibility of paying the bills not only of the church, but his members were going through one of the toughest economic times in the churches history which was short lived. Robert prayed and prayed asking God to intervene on behalf of his people, but there was no noticeable answer. I'm implying that God did not answer, I'm saying Robert could not see the answer due to the church's financial difficulties. One day an older female pastor came to Roberts new start up church to announce how she had found favor in Gods eyes and wanted to share the blessing. She told the congregation how she was approached by an investor who was willing to pour tons of money into her ministry and I would not cost her a thing. The pastor went on to say how they had been working on the plans to expand her ministry which was small like Roberts at the time. What she said or testified to seemed like an answer to her prayers. The congregation was moved and erupted in spontaneous praises and with a youthful jubilance they were expecting God to move in their church next. Within a few weeks the pastor came back and asked Roberts church to join her and meeting with her new business partner who would take the church to the next level. If you haven't already notice I said Roberts church because she respected some of the older members in his church just not him because they had no personal relationship and she thought Robert was new to the ministry and didn't know a thing yet.

Robert reluctantly agreed to meet at her church and hear what was said by the new investors. When they arrived Robert noticed two men standing in nice suits and fine jewelry who seem to have a lot of documents with them, as the meeting went on the men asked each person to tell a little about themselves and what their dreams and visions was for the church. Everyone seemed excited that they finally had a chance to tell and bring forth the ministry God had given them. Robert did admit he was exited at first, but the more he listen to the finely dressed men the more he noticed their presentation offer no real plan of action. They talked about faith and partnering with there company and how many churches they helped up and down the east coast, and never provided any real names of churches. You must understand the internet was still new and Robert was using that famous company that announced you had mail every day, so there was no way to immediately check for references. Robert seemed to be the only pastor in the meeting who was asking question that got deflected by answers such as "you have to have faith" and "we have done this before" as they held up a stack of documents but never allowed anyone to view them. The men asked for investments or seed money and the church would be contacted and a blueprint would be drawn up in a few days with a contract, but we must invest today. With everyone else seeming to support the idea and the investment Robert announced his congregation would not be participating which upset many of them. Robert received the backlash and the old silent treatment from some of his members. They wonder how he could walk away from such a blessing, beside the pastor who brought them to the meeting could vouch for them and she has the paperwork to prove it. A few months later Robert later discover that the two men who conducted the meeting quickly disappeared with the pastor's money, hopes and dreams of the congregation. Leaving the pastor to explain what had happened and why she didn't see this coming. Even though Robert was right in not investing in the company he never received any apology or pat on the back for saving them from losing money. There are those who seek to profit in the name of God, never loving the sheep or have their interest at heart. This has happened in the old testament and the new, now I understand what Jesus meant when he said to be wise as a serpent or be so to speak and quick to listen. Don't be discouraged by wicked men, they are not only in political power they are also sitting in the pews, this I why we must stay focused on the person of Jesus Christ and put our trust only in him.

COVER ME

I remember as a child growing up in a small community where everyone knew everyone's parents. Its seems cliché but in the 70s if you told your parents I'm going over to James house they immediately knew who he was and his entire family tree. Back then neighbors took care of each other's kids and if you stepped out of line you better believe they would correct you without hesitation or fear of what your parents would say. It didn't matter if you went from one side of town to another your name would tell anyone who you were and how to fine you nearest relative. Being married to a city girl I have found that we grew up in two entirely different communities. There was not the level of trust in the inner city compared to our small town. The wife and I sit by the fire and talk about how we grew up and the difficulty we faced as children. She would tell stories of having to clean, being spanked, different types of food she ate and didn't enjoy one bit. I often find it hilarious some of the things she talks about like being in the house all day or getting her hair straighten with a straightening comb for Easter. When its my turn to tell my stories her continence changes, because it's hard for her to believe we grew up poor. I can tell those stories because to me it was a way of life, not something to be ashamed of. My mother and father did the best they could and always surrounded us with love which continuous cover our condition. Some new younger parents believe if I just give my children this toy or this phone, they will be happy and love me more. It's a sad mistake that they don't often learn until later in life, I have found through my studies in psychology and helping raise family members that what children want and need the most is their parents. Growing up in a two-parent home I depended on my parents for everything, even though we didn't' have much I wouldn't change a thing. Back to my wife and her continence changing because of how I grew up. When I reminisce about not having simple things like running water, cutting wood with an ax in the winter time, sleeping with your clothes on to stay warm at night, among many other things I could talk about but out of respect for my wonderful parents and time, I will not. I remember my mother making thick winter blankets out of old clothes and stuffing it with more old clothes too keep us warm in the winter. She always made sure we were covered before going to sleep. Until this day I still haven't slept under anything that thick, and warm. No, it wasn't pretty, and it wasn't something you purchase from a store or yard sale, but if you understood how warm it was, you could understand its value. Looking back in time I could see some of same patterns on the beds of other relatives, whom my grandmother made covers for. My mother always showed how much she loved us there were times when we did not have a washing machine or couldn't go to the laundry mat due to the distance and transportation. Mother would wash clothes by hand for four children and her husband, just to make sure we had something clean. She was a wonderful woman who never got the praise or accolades she deserved. I often wonder how she could take a few random things in the kitchen and make the best meals ever, they were so good we would get two or three plates if possible. Now that I'm grown, I try to duplicate some of the meals she cooked and pass on the love she showed us to my children and grandchildren. Mother helped me understand by her actions how God keeps us covered even though we don't appreciate him for all that he does. The bible says, "he allows the sun to shine on the righteous as well as the unrighteous". Imagine if we were judge immediately for everything we did wrong or how many times you blamed God for a bad event. You would not be here today reading this book. It was because he covered you when being a sinner, rebellious, angry, fornicator, drug addict, ill moral, proud, unholy we are here today. I can look at many events in my life from a child until an adult where I should not be on this earth today and there is no other explanation but by the grace of God. I know we have all heard it in church before, it becomes real when you're a policeman chasing someone through the projects at 3:00 am in the morning and they pull a gun which you never saw until it was pointed at you. It becomes real when your laying in the hospital emergency room because your diabetic and haven't had your insulin in three months, the doctors wonder how you even walked in the door. God becomes real when you're in a strange city surrounded by people who want to kill you for your faith, but God covered you. I must tell you about Kevin before we leave this section. Kevin was a newlywed who was building a productive life with his wife. They didn't have the newest things in life, but he did have enough to keep the jones in sight, that is until he lost his job, he had been on for past eight years. Kevin being the man of the house and the only provider lost faith in God, the church and all of humanity. Kevin had spent most of his life in the church paying tithes and giving an offering, he worked in the local ministry without complaining. Kevin considered himself a man of faith, if the pastor said it then we must trust that God is using them. When Kevin lost his job, it seemed those who were in the church he supported no longer wanted to be around him. There were no more calls from church member, no more words of encouragement, he felt abandoned by the church and God. Kevin no longer felt the need to go to church and be around a lot of phony people who say they love God but can't support you when in the time of need. When the food ran out and Kevin had no money or transportation because his car was repossessed, Kevin believed he couldn't get any lower. He was looking inside of an empty refrigerator with a head of rotting lettuce an gnats nothing in the pantry except a small bag of rice and Brunswick stew. Kevin thought to himself "ill make this at least it's something" and I want to have to ask those so call Christians for anything. With no hope insight he made his last meal which he forced down and began to think about how much of a failure he was. While Kevin sat in his home alone something was eating at his conscience, he couldn't let those nats stay in the refrigerator. Kevin got up and pull the refrigerator to the patio outside and began to clean it with brillo pads, bleach and a garden hose. I think it was a miracle itself that Kevin moved an entire refrigerator from the kitchen to the outside patio by himself. Kevin didn't know why he wanted to clean the refrigerator so bad, but he did without complaining. Kevin said he then felt a sense of peace as he move the refrigerator back inside of the kitchen. Kevin said as he laid there on the bed trying to figure out his next move, he heard a car pull up in the driveway. Kevin said he looked out the window and saw a familiar car one he had seen at his house in sometime. The car stopped and out came Kevin's wife from the passenger side, Kevin then went to lay back down on the bed. It was only his wife and old church member. Kevin did not feel like entertaining any company at the time in fact he was feeling quite resentful to those in the church. Kevin heard the front door open and the wife come in then the old church member. Kevin's wife seemed to be in a quite joyous mood due to her loud happy demeanor. As she entered and exited the front door several times Kevin wonder why she is going in and out, the only thing he could see was the cold air going out the door and he couldn't pay the bill now. In a moment of anger Kevin got out of the bed determined to tell his wife how much money she was costing him. He walked out of the bedroom into the kitchen to his surprise the kitchen was full of grocery bags of food. Its was more food than Kevin had seen in months at his house. With his mouth open and eyes looking in disbelief Kevin asked his wife, where did all of this come from? She responded from the old church member, his wife explained it was on his heart to help us, as soon as he got his social security check. Kevin asked again why to which she responded because he likes us, and God laid it on his heart. Kevin like Job had learned to trust God in the midst of adversity, and not to look with the natural eye but with the spiritual eye. God never abandon Kevin in his time of need in fact he was directing and perfecting him. Kevin learned not to look to men for all of his needs but trust the God who has the cattle on a thousand hills. Kevin had to learn we must empty out all the trust we have in ourselves and totally rely on God who is the author and finisher of our faith. There will be times in your life when God doesn't talk to you or reveal his plans for you, its during these times we must understand God is still in control. King David expressed it well when he said I have never seen the righteous forsaken nor his seed begging bread. Will you allow him to cover you today?

TIME TO HEAL

I know reading some of these stories can be quiet discouraging at time, but that is not my goal. I hope you understand that you're not the only one who faced adversity in the church, countless others have and some never came back. I have heard stories of people who find more love and acceptance in the street than in the church. Its sad when people feel its easier to live in strife rather than give it all to God. Do they have a legitimate complaint, I strongly agree they do? Through the years as I was growing up, the things that was said to new converts would make your skin crawl. Things such as you can't wear that to Gods house now that your saved or delivered. You can't be around those type of people because you're a child of God and you have to be an example; they will take what little strength or faith you already have. The church today and the church back then has made a great mistake in trying to force people to live holy as soon as they are converted to what we refer to as christiany. We forget that it is God through his word and the holy spirit that will complete the change if men get out of his way and allow him to be God and God alone. We forget that it wasn't any thing that we have done to convert hearts to him, it's them seeming themselves as guilty sinners, who have sinned against God and God only. The church is guilty of trying to convert people for its own glory, whether it's for financial, social, political gain, all conversions should give the glory to God and him only. When the apostle converted thousands to Christianity through the preaching and teaching of Jesus Christ, they never told the people you belong under this particular ministry now that you have received Christ here. They never encouraged people to stay and adhere strictly to the teachings of the Apostle Paul, Peter, James, or John, they encouraged believers to seek a foundation in Jesus Christ and grow in grace and the knowledge of our lord and savior Jesus Christ. It was not encouraged to stay with one Apostle over another. Today we see churches constraining new converts to stay in place where they were converted. I wonder sometimes what they would say to the scripture where one plants, another waters, its God who gives the increase. It's not our job to hold people, its our job to show them the grace of God. If we hold them and try to control, their lives we become nothing more than a cult. Even God allowed man to leave him time after time in the old testament and each time after they repented, he was there to restore them. Love that is forced or controlled is not love at all, in some cases we can call it by another name abuse. Healing isn't always easy neither does it happen overnight, it can take months if not years to overcome the smallest infraction. In my experience over the years, there were many who could never return to the church because of the hurt. They were expected to heal overnight and see a perfect God, who loved them, and everything would be ok. Wrong! Christians quickly forget that even though we have a heavenly mind and spirit we are still trapped in this thing that God hates which is called flesh. As long a we are in this flesh we will be subject to all the hurts and pains that come with it. There is no separation of the flesh and spirit until Jesus comes back to claim his bride. The bible even shows us this amazing truth when it teaches us to put our flesh under subjection every day, because there's a constant war going on in these bodies. Oh, how I wish it was easy to cast of the terrestrial and put on the celestial, then I show people you can't hurt what you can't touch. I thank God for his son Jesus who died and suffered for my sins, he felt all the pain of a natural man in his flesh. The amazing part is even though he had visible scars from a traumatic experience he also showed that you can heal. No matter what you have been through or where you have been or done, you can heal. Some people may need professional help, and there is nothing wrong with that, go where you can get your healing, it's not always in the local church. Are you ready to be healed?

UNEXPECTED ANGELS

I have heard stories of the Arch Angel Michael and people throughout my life telling stories of being in the presence of angels who simply disappear or are never heard of again. These meetings tend to border on the supernatural, where God stepped in and rescued you when no one else was around. I believe that God does still work miracles in our lives today sometimes we miss what he's doing because of science and our on dependency on self. I have learned over the course of many years of being in law enforcement to look and appreciate the hand of God in everyday occurrences. I'm not going to tell too many old police stories, but I do find it amazing to see how some people or babies walk away form car crashes that are complete totaled without a scratch. To see a shooting victim out of the hospital the next day, or a pedestrian struck by a car or train and still live to talk about it. These people I believe have hidden angels, because there is no other explanation of why he or she is still alive. There are other angles that we never take notice of every day, I'm going to discuss one of my hidden angels, which I did not notice until God removed the scales from my eyes. While going through some difficult times in my life there was one angel who was placed in my life for my physical protection and to help my wavering faith in the church return to normal whatever that is. The angel I'm talking about jokingly said you going to put me in your book to which I replied do you have any horror stories. For the purpose of this book I will call him by another name Dalton. I know Dalton did not mean what he said about the book because he's not that type of person. What I learned from Dalton reaffirmed my faith in Gods ability to use anyone at anytime for any reason. I'm not saying Dalton is someone who we should exalt to a position of saint hood in a biblical cannon, no he has flaws just like anyone else and he himself would quickly admit it. He's just that honest and straight forward. Dalton is a big man the kind of guy you would hate to see in a fight with anyone, if you did the only thing you could do was pray for the other person, because he is to big and strong to bed pull of someone. I thank God I never made Dalton that mad. Yes, on a couple occasion I did ruffle his feathers, but it was nothing we could not get past. The thing about Dalton is just be honest with him if you screwed up just admit it and move on, he's going to tell you what he thinks, like I said earlier he's just that honest. If you focus on Daltons size and scary physique you will miss 90 percent of who he really is. On the outside he is scary as a silverback gorilla, on the inside he's the most giving person you could ever meet. What do I mean by that? Dalton is that person if you're hungry he's going to feed you, if your naked he's going to get you something to wear. If your struggling with life he's going to call and make every attempt to help you find a solution. If you're a stranger and you leave your children at his home, he will treat them exactly like his, no difference. If it's on Christmas day guess what your kids are getting gifts also, even though Dalton is a big man I believe his heart is larger than his stature. Dalton is that guy who never brags about anything he has or the many titles or positions he has held in other companies. He doesn't talk about his money; he doesn't talk about his kids getting all (A's) in school or how they are being recruited by different colleges. He doesn't talk about his volunteer work he does in the community helping and providing for disadvantaged children out of his own pocket. He doesn't talk about the famous people he knows or how he works multilabel jobs not for his family but too help other people. Dalton is what I call a hidden angel, he doesn't talk about what church he goes to or what was the last sermon he heard. He will tell you how he was raised in the church, and his faith in God. Dalton has protected me from myself when I was having medical issues and didn't even know it. He's that person who said hey you need medical attention right now when no one else could see I was having medical issues. He's that person who would call me on the phone and say hey you need to fix this with your staff right now, most people would take that as an insult, I learned with Dalton Listen to him. Why? Because he's telling not to be mean but to help you, and usually he's right. The thing about hidden angels is they don't belong to any church or recognize any specific denomination they do what they do because they fear God and its right. Dalton doesn't ask anyone for anything, but he is constantly giving to others without any recognition, in fact if I mention his real name in this book, I would get an earful from him. He does everything from his heart and doesn't seek any recognition from men. I wonder how many churches could use someone like Dalton in their ministry who is already working with children, the homeless, and other programs. I wanted to recruit Dalton for my church's ministry, but God said no, this is where he is need and is being used outside of the church wall. I understood then it's the hidden angles who can't work in any organized institution, they are out on the streets for a reason. This is where Dalton is the most effective on the dirty streets with his people as he calls them. I said to myself wow what if the church took this attitude of being on the streets with their people no matter what condition they are in. Looking at Dalton restored my faith in the church invisible, I mean those who are known of God and believe in him. Jesus healed many people, and, in some cases, he told the people not to tell anyone. There are other cases he told the people to show themselves to the chief priest or scribes so that they can believe. Today it seems the church has become commercial and religious, if you're not under a covering or ministry you are out of the will of God. To them I say, I read in the bible where the disciple was worried about others using Jesus name to cast out demons and perform miracles. Jesus said leave them alone. Let us pray for and thank God for the Dalton's who do his will and restore the faith of those who have been let down by the organized church.

THE DOCTORS IN

If you have ever visited the south in some places you can drive down a road and ride for miles without seeing a house, gas station, store or even another person. One thing I love about the south is you could enjoy nature and all its beauty without being interrupted by cars, television, cell phones, or other people. It feels like your connected to your environment and all of your senses can come alive immediately, small things such as sounds and smell you never noticed before, but now they are so vivid and clear. The smell of a honeysuckle can be so sweet or that of a muscadine vine who has just dropped its fruit. Even though it's a thing of beauty to me, there is always something that you may be missing and not even know it. While driving down those beautiful roads which seem to go on without end it's hard to imagine how someone could survive without the modern world ever touching their lives. Well it depends on what you're accustom too and what you feel your missing out of life. As a child I never really considered the idea of needing a doctor for anything, because a lot of old medicine and holistic healing was passed down from generation to generation. The majority of the time instead of going into town to see a doctor, my parents could talk to their parents or someone who was and elder in the community who could give a solution to almost anything. Wisdom can only go so far if its no kissed by knowledge. When a child has broken his bone its time to send him to the doctor and not try any remedies at home. There are viruses out there that can and have killed many due to lack of education and understanding in our local communities. I'm not suggesting that God didn't provide man with wisdom "however" he did us the ability to study the human body and mind, not for his benefit but for ours. Each year I watch the news and see how a new strand of virus, bacteria, or disease has killed thousands of people and seem to be getting out of control before some cure or new treatment is discovered. Without our scientific community constantly discover new medicine and treatments for disease, we would lose millions of people each year. Do I believe God can heal anything "Yes", at the same time I believe doctors have a purpose also? Many people go through life hurting and sometime hemorrhaging for a traumatic spiritual event, and they come to the church looking for healing. Many leave disillusions or feeling as if God did not hear them or they don't deserve too be healed. When in fact they go to church and won't even acknowledge what the symptoms of their sickness is. Can you imagine going to your local doctor and saying I'm sick you figure it out you're the doctor, then walking out with medication for your sickness. Many of us go to God and tell him we are sick and tired of our lives, and tired of living the way we do each week, but we want tell him what that is. What are you trying to hide? He already knows, its his desire for you to have an open and honest dialogue with him. People tend to have an excuse for every situation, and example is if he knows why tell him. If that's the example you want to use allow me to use this example, if you have ever had children and they do something wrong such as lie, break something steal, you want them to be able to come to you without any hesitation and confess what they did. Many times, you already know, you just want that open dialogue and them to realize no matter what you are still here for them. Not to say their want be any repercussions for their actions, what it does provide them with is your knowledge and wisdom to a sometimes-simple problem. As a parent we must teach our children how to resolve some problems and allow them space to grow by figuring out others. God allows us the space to communicate with him and grow on our own. We can't say God heal me of this physical disease when what we really need is a psychological and spiritual cleanse from all of the junk, we have stored up for years that's now affecting our health. Many years ago, I weighed 295lbs and my weight according to science was supposed to be 185lbs base on my height, age, bmi. I could have said God heal me from all this excess weight I put on over the years. Well a strange thing happened I went to my primary care physician and he said I was prediabetic. I really didn't think anything of it, because diabetes ran in my family and I understood the signs and symptoms of the disease. A few weeks later will conducting an annual physical for my job they did the same test and said you are a full-blown diabetic with blood sugar so high I could not be read on a meter. The doctor asked me how I felt, I told her no different than any other day, I'm not tired, sluggish, thirsty, urinating a lot, I feel fine. She wanted to put me in the hospital that day, but I reassured her I was fine and continued to work as usual. I could have prayed lord deliver me from the diabetes and felt abandon if God didn't do it. Well I didn't ask God for deliverance that year. What I did have to face was the problem of how I got this big. After considering all that I have went through in life with, church, family, friends, jobs. I realized I was an emotional eater, every time I got bothered by something, I would have to have chocolate or something sweet. I put on so much weight so fast, I went from a size 36 pants to 48-50 all because I didn't want to deal with my personal issues. God allowed me to destroy myself physically so he could save me physically and spiritually. My wife convinced me to go to the doctor where they found, not only did I have out of control diabetes, I had a heart problem that could have killed me in a few years. I was a ticking time bomb and it took a God, a good wife and diabetes to save my life. Today I have this disease under control and hope to kill it one day with faith, exercise, diet. My heart is fine, and I have learned how to properly express most of my feelings (I'm a work in progress). I write this so that you can understand that if I had stayed that way and waited for God to do something and not acknowledge what was really going on with me, by listening to the body he gave me years ago I would not be writing this book right now. I had deep emotional and spiritual problem I never wanted to deal with and just bush them under the rug. God is talking through the little things are you really listening, or will it take something dramatic to get and hold your attention.

TIME TO COME HOME

I know its easier said than done when someone invites you to trust God again. You feel as if they are telling you to forget all the pain you have experienced over the years if not decades. They want you to forget and sweep it under the rug and start new again, well its not all ways that easy, you have to acknowledge the hurt, pain, disappointment, rejection, humiliation, disgrace, rejection or whatever you have experienced and let it go. You have been holding on to things that are destroying you mentally, physically, spiritually, and psychologically. I understand that it feels hard, and the two most common feelings are revenge and blame. You must understand, we cannot control everything that someone else has done to you or someone else. I mention this before, being human means your going to make mistakes, they were human and made some big mistakes. That doesn't mean you should compromise your relationship with God, or you give up on him. Think of a few people in the bible who did something crazy like Jonah who refused to preach and ran all because he wanted revenge and didn't feel they were worthy of Gods forgiveness. What about Jobs wife who was the closest person to him in his life. Instead of encouraging him she wanted him to curse God and die, talking about a heart break. What about Hosea who took a harlot and married her, cleaned her name and image up, had a family with her, just to left by her and she went back into prostitution. There are countless stories like these in the bible and in the lives of many of your television evangelicals. At the end of the day they had to endure, because God had a greater plan for them and the ministry to which they were called. You will never know the completion of Gods plan for your life if you never return home. I must say this again never look at man for all your solutions it is God is waiting to commune with you in your secret place. Men will and have failed you time and time again, God has never failed you. Understand the difference, there were those who went in the name of Jesus but were not sent of Jesus, and when the disciple brought this to Jesus attention, he said leave them alone. Yes, people will make mistakes, but who is making the bigger mistake them or you're by separating yourself from the only one who will never leave you. Like the father of the prodigal son he is standing there waiting for you to return home with no condemnation. He is ready to cloth you in his love and present you too the world as a son or daughter. He will never ask you where you have been or what you did wrong while you were gone, he only wants you too take your place by his side. It is my hope and prayer that you make the decision to return home and stop living a life that below his expectation and yours. You were created to make a difference in this world, want you commit fulfilling your destiny in Christ. He's waiting for you my brother and sister just to come back home. Come.

Printed in the United States
By Bookmasters